I0789838

Covered: Six Steps To Design The Perfect Book Cover

Andrew J. Becker

Stephanie Summers

ISBN: 1975746317
ISBN-13: 978-1975746315

v

CONTENTS

INTRODUCTION

This guide will be just as brief and straight-forward as this introduction, and full disclosure: I'm not a writer. I love images, drawings, graphics, and pretty much anything else I can stare at to avoid working. Expressing myself through design, photography, and the occasional interpretive dance I do while cooking dinner, has always come more naturally.

For this book, I wanted to share my insights, thought process, and general ramblings that I go through for each cover I design. As with everything comes a learning curve and practice definitely does not make perfect, but it does help you figure out which keys pop off easily when you slam your keyboard.

I hope you are able to finish this book with your perfect book cover in hand and a best seller on the shelves. So please enjoy the guide and remember that this paper also makes wonderful paper airplanes to annoy anyone with twenty feet of you.

JUDGE, JURY, AND BESTSELLER

All of the fonts, the colors, the labels, the bottle shapes. Walking up and down the aisles of any wine shop I find myself near, I am mesmerized by the variety of stylistic choices, some for the better and some not so much. My eyes constantly jumping from one to the next, all the while knowing that no matter my opinions on the label, I have no idea what awaits beneath the cork. Obvious clues on the label guide my efforts in the right direction but then the mind games settle in:

> *This looks good, but what if they had a bad year and are trying to cover it up with a good label? Did they exhaust all of their efforts in to the bottle design and leave the wine lackluster? Or maybe they had an amazing year and want to draw you in with a beautiful label! That's gotta be it! They're so proud of what you're about to enjoy that they took the time and care to create something wonderful from shelf to glass. Or maybe…*

Long story short: My beautiful wife ends up dragging me out of the store as I cling to ten bottles with sweaty palms. This unnecessary crisis I endure a few times more often than I'd like to admit has taught me an important lesson. One that this chapter will help you to understand, emphasize, and utilize: **judge a book by its cover.** You only get one chance to make a first impression. No matter how wonderful the story or innovative the ideas in your book are, what if no one picks it up off the shelf? Making your first- or millionth sale starts when someone sees your cover.

Learning from the mistakes of others is a skill that few have, one that I'm still working on myself. *The stove is hot, but how will I know…?* Luckily for me, and maybe you, there are other ways we can learn and grow at others expense.

Expense, quite literally. Book publishers spend hundreds of millions of dollars each year researching, designing, and testing book cover designs for every genre, style, and market. And you can access all of the results from their budget bursting research for free. Walk in to any book store or search on Amazon. Not to discredit the works of best selling authors but the content only matters if someone is interested enough to pick the book off of a shelf or click on the Amazon listing.

One of the first book covers I worked on was for a friend releasing a niche exercise guide. *Oh yea, I know what's on the cover of an exercise book! Muscles, weights, sweat, grunge!* After my second or third mock-up, I was feeling pretty satisfied with myself and thought I'd take a peek at some of the best selling exercise books to compare and get some ideas for colors or typography. About twenty-five pages deep in to my Amazon search I realized that the best sellers looked nothing like what I had originally created. Confused, I kept searching, page after page until I finally found a few similar covers selling maybe a few copies each month.

I frantically started comparing some of the top sellers to the ones that weren't so top. Based on the descriptions, the samples, the reviews, the pricing, I couldn't find a real difference. With the exception of the cover.

I decided to take a few covers from each group and compare them; what I found seems so obvious now. The best sellers were bright, happy, inspiring, and clean. Quite different from what I thought what make a powerful and top selling cover. Understanding the content of the book is vital to creating a cover that uniquely and properly represents your book. *But!* Make it sell. Your best tool to do that is your cover.

Find the comparable best sellers to your book, print out the covers or buy a few of them. Make notes, compare what each has that is unique and design elements that they share. We'll break down the elements further later on, but seeing each cover objectively as a buyer is important at this stage. Here's a few tricks I've picked up analyzing covers over the years:

- Put the cover on a shelf across the room. What colors stand out? What can you read? Is one slightly larger?

- Put all of the covers on the same shelf across the room. Which elements make certain covers stand out?

- Set them all out on a shelf or table and walk past them a few times. Which stands out in the corner of your eye?

- Place them on a book shelf with the spines out. Do certain books stand out more this way? Can you read them? Do they emphasize a certain color?

- Leave them on your shelf or table for a few days. Do any stand out more over time? Do they seem out of place? Do you want to pick a certain one up?

- Don't forget about online shopping! Click on all of the pages, the descriptions, compare them on different sites. Which covers work well on the computer screen? What about on your phone? Can you read the title?

You can do all of these things without leaving the book store. Maybe you'll get a few strange looks, but at the end of the day, but who's going to be selling the most books? You. They'll just regret not getting your autograph when they had the chance. It can be tempting to envision your title and name on the cover, but this stage is all about identifying the elements that make up a consistent and top-selling book cover.

• Make a list of five elements that the top selling covers within your genre have in common.

• Make a list of two elements that each cover has that are unique from the others.

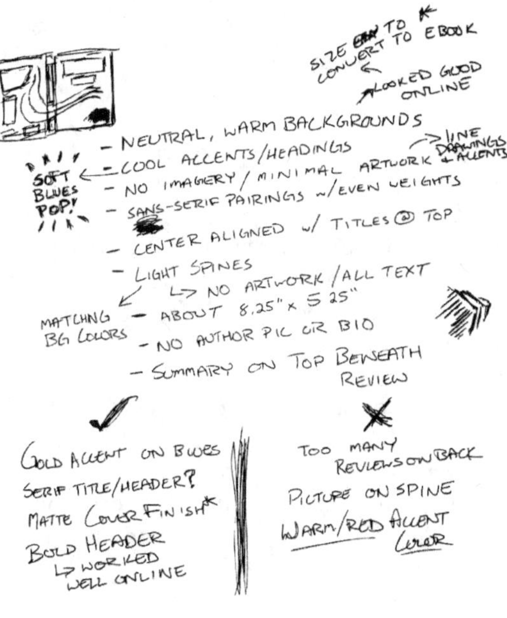

A page from my book of cover design notes and example of my horrible handwriting.

This list will be the **foundation** for your cover design. I've developed dozens of designs for every book I've worked on and no matter how unique they become, they all work and sell because they follow this basic foundation.

SIZE MATTERS

Now that your foundation is laid out, let's get building. From here on we'll be breaking down the specifics of the most important and universal aspects of your book cover. This really just means more pictures; lucky you (and me).

Forget what they say, size does matter. The only limit on your book cover design? How big, or small, it is. From your **foundation** notes, identify the most commonly used sizes, as well as some outliers. Like we discussed earlier on, publishers have invested heavily on figuring out the absolute best way to design and sell a book, including the measurements of those sheets of paper.

It is important to utilize these dimensions when choosing yours but don't forget that it is also has to work with what information you've got inside yours. Many of the measurements are proportional to each other so you can stay within the same relative size but ensure your inside layout nestles neatly within.

Traditional paperbacks cover most types of books and they loosely follow the 2:3 ratio that is considered standard. Most on-demand printers offer these sizes as their least expensive. The dimension is versatile and commonly used throughout most genres and styles.

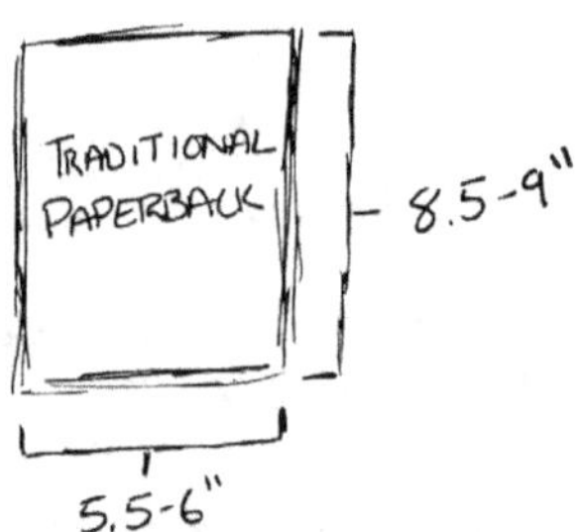

A few tricks and variations that are common within genres:

Self-help & motivational 6 - 7" x 8 - 10"
Short novels and memoirs 5.25 - 5.5" x 8 - 8.5"
Longer novels 6" x 9"
General non-fiction 6 - 7" x 9 - 10"

References, manuals, and workbooks are typically larger and closer to the square (1:1) ratio. Usually featuring images or diagrams; it is common here to let the interior book design determine your cover dimensions.

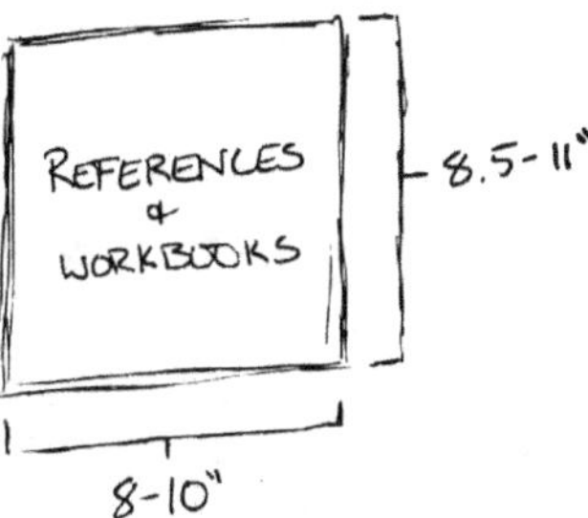

Art, photography, and coffee table books are able to print in nearly any size you'd like. Traditionally, they tend to follow the square (1:1) ratio but there is no standard. To keep printing costs down, stay between 5" and 12" on all sides.

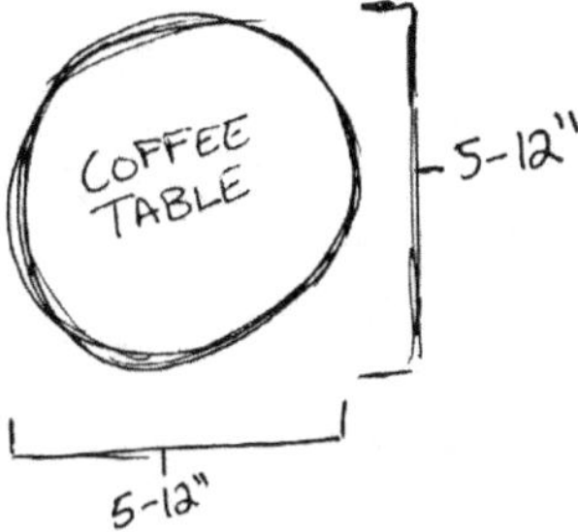

Determining your book size is the first thing I do for any project. Establishing that boundary gives you a clearer frame to start within and determine what is really necessary to display on your cover. Many self publishers want to incorporate as many elements in to their cover design as possible, thinking that it will help sell their book. In turn it becomes cluttered, busy, and overwhelming and leads buyers to move on.

The goal is to get your book in to as many people's hands as possible. Setting the dimensions early will help you determine what is important to include and what is distracting your buyer.

COVER YOURSELF

To the drawing board! We've got the shape of our book, now we can fill it in. Selecting cover art can feel like a shot in the dark if you have no direction. Luckily for us, we've got a pretty good treasure map to a successful design in our **foundation**. To figure out which road you're on, we'll break down a few of the most popular cover art styles and discuss ways you can design something unique and effective.

This step can be daunting for many people looking to design their own book cover but focus on developing a few alternates using one, or a mix, of the cover art styles. Designers will often utilize placeholder images or artwork just to get a sense of what the final design will look like. This is a great and time saving technique that lets you work out any sizing or layout issues without fully committing to one particular design.

Keep moving forward. If you're stuck going back and forth between two ideas, bag them up and let's go! Explore each option to see which will be a good fit for your book and genre, and then when you're ready, we'll see you in typography!

Keeping it **minimal** is always a good and relatively easier route. This style has been growing in popularity recently across many genres and works well both online and in print. Lacking artwork or imagery can help save some money but it's important to invest your time in the next two steps to create something that comes across as a bestseller.

A classic look that draws the focus to the title and creates a clean and minimal feel. Utilize a smart color choice for the background or text to add a little more pop. Negative space, good use of typeface, and playful text placement will draw your audience in.

Common uses for this style include novels and short stories, literature collections, and references.

Say cheese! Photography is another growing trend in book cover design and something that can be easily utilized in your design. Within different genres, different photography styles will be more popular, especially among the top selling books. Professional photography will come at an increased cost but is something that will be worth it to stand your book out and build the immediate connection with your target audience.

Photography can be utilized in a variety of ways, whether featuring an individual, a location, or a conceptual idea. All of these styles will reach out to and connect with your audience differently. Stock imagery is a great, and sometimes more affordable, resource to help bring your ideas to life and explore various options easily.

A few common genres that utilize photography are biographies, self-help, motivational, and industry resources.

Featuring artwork in your design can be a great middle ground between photography and a minimal cover. The costs tend to be more moderate than photography, depending on your ideas and usage. There are a variety of styles included in this route so it's important to take note of commonalities in your foundations cover art to build on. Reach out to local artists for commissioned pieces or license an existing work for your cover. You have a few options here that can add individuality to your design while maintaining your strong foundation.

The artwork route is the most versatile and conceptual way to add a visual element to your cover design. Artwork can serve to symbolize a theme, create a mood, reference a historical period, or provide your cover with a unique and effective feature to draw the audiences eye.

This cover style is used commonly for many books and can be utilized at varying scale and depth, suiting your design best.

TYPICAL TYPOGRAPHY TIPS

Far from it. One of the most underrated art forms in the world: typography. It is used every single day, no matter who you are, what you're doing, or where you're going. And could possibly be the most important design element of your book cover.

Typography style can vary wildly from genre to genre, and even within genres. Whether being utilized as the cover art itself or just listing the title and author, choosing the right style and pairings is vital. We'll continue to use our **foundation** to identify the common typographical styles and break down a variety of font pairings to create a cover that is unique and smart.

Elements that make typography pairings successful can be hard to identify but easy to duplicate. The styles used on the best sellers we analyzed in the beginning were selected for a specific reason. Choosing the perfect fonts for your cover doesn't have to be hard work; take advantage of the research they've done and utilize the results.

These pairings are only a sampling, there are infinite possibilities but these are the ones I've found most common, most effective, and most efficient. Most of the typefaces listed are relatively easy to find online but costs can vary depending on your usage. Use these examples as inspiration or duplicate them directly, it's up to you.

A Wondrous Journey

through time and space

A large and airy, lightweight sans-serif combined with a smaller, lowercase transitional serif italicized.

lightweight sans-serif

Roboto (thin)
Avenir Next (ultra light)
Gotham (light)

italic transitional serif

Times New Roman (italic)
Hoefler Text (italic)
Baskerville (italic)

The Power of Passion

A Guide to Finding Yours

A heavy slab serif accented by a lighter transitional serif.

heavy slab serif

Rockwell (bold)
Soho
Alfa Slab

light transitional serif

Baskerville
Georgia
Bell MT

The Days Are Long

and the years are short

A heavier brush script font paired with a transitional serif.

heavy brush script	**transitional serif**
Ballpark	Hoefler Text
Marguerite	Garamond
Sign Painter	Times New Roman

Looking Up

FROM A DIFFERENT PERSPECTIVE

A handwritten script with a heavier, capitalized sans-serif.

handwritten script	**heavy sans-serif**
Honey Script	Montserrat (bold)
Honilad	Ubuntu (bold)
Frenchpress	Avenir Next (bold)

A GREAT ADVENTURE

and the lessons never learned

A capitalized, geometric sans-serif paired with a light, condensed sans-serif.

heavy geometric sans-serif

Roboto (bold)
Avenir Next (heavy)
Arial (black)

light condensed sans-serif

Avenir Next (condensed)
Future (condensed medium)
Ubuntu (condensed)

LOCK & KEY

finding the perfect pair

A medium, capitalized slab serif typeface with a light, simple, handwritten script.

medium slab serif

Made Likes Slab
Rockwell
Citizen Slab

light handwritten script

Avenir Hand (condensed)
Five Minutes
Frenchpress

BUILD IT UP
to tear it down

A capitalized, modern serif and a light, geometric sans-serif.

modern serif

Bodoni 72
Didot (bold)
Voor

light geometric sans-serif

Roboto (thin)
Gotham (light)
Adam

A City of Light
comes alive at night

A heavier sans-serif accented by an italicized, medium serif.

heavy sans-serif

Montserrat (semi bold)
Ubuntu (bold)
Gill Sans

medium serif

Times New Roman (italic)
Garamond (italic)
Hoefler Text (italic)

Pro-tip: there are often less expensive alternatives to many popular fonts if you find something you like that's a bit out of your budget. Be certain that you have the proper licenses for any fonts you choose!

Alrighty, what else is on the list? Sizing? Check. Cover art? Check. Typography? Check. Well, color me impressed, only a few more things.

COLOR BY NUMBERS

Making us feel a certain way, literally. Color emotion theory is another design element used all around us every single day and we barely notice. Well, consciously we barely notice. Our brain is a mysterious place.

Publishers and designers have researched the effects of colors used on book covers and I'm sure you'll notice a pattern from your **foundation** research too. We'll lay out the basics behind it so you can understand but following the lead of the top sellers is a good direction to head in. You can utilize the colors in your design to reach out to your audience, get the book in their hands, and get them to buy.

Similar to your typeface pairing, you'll want to stick with a color palette throughout your entire cover design. Adobe Color (www.color.adobe.com) is a fantastic tool to explore popular color palettes easily and develop your own using presets or custom tools.

The amount of colors you choose may vary but a general design rule is 1-3 colors not including black and white. Now, let's build the backbone of this design (yes, that was a spine joke).

white	**grey**	**black**
innocent	timeless	power
clean	practical	strength
airy	official	streamline
neutral	sophisticated	authority
pure		mourning

red	**orange**	**yellow**
romantic	energetic	warning
passionate	change	intensity
warmth	growth	frustration
life	happiness	optimism
comfort	stimulating	hunger

green	**blue**	**purple**
natural	security	royal
calming	cold	elegant
prosperity	loyal	respect
fertility	focused	mystery
harmony	truthful	wisdom

pink	**brown**
loving	reliable
endearing	organic
gentle	stable
softness	sadness

BABY GOT BACK(BONE)

Time to flip! There was a reason we checked out the spine and back cover when we were looking at the other top sellers, I wasn't just wasting your time. Most of the time, people will see the cover we've so excellently designed first. *But, what if they don't? What about the spine? What about the precious back cover?*

Luckily, these designs tend to be a little more universal but still important to focus on and create something that is consistent with your front cover and informative to the buyer. Depending on your book dimensions and length, your spine size will vary so it's important to check with your printer before choosing a design to go with. The two most common and effective spine layouts will utilize elements from your front cover style.

If you've chosen to go with a full cover photograph or artwork, you can decide whether you want the imagery to wrap around the spine or cut off at the edge. Both styles are common and can be used effectively throughout most genres. It's important to experiment with putting text over the imagery or artwork and determining it's legibility. If the artwork or text is too busy together, don't force them. Some designers insist that having your title and information on the spine is vital but there are many examples of best sellers using artwork or imagery that is intriguing enough to stand out without text.

Artwork wrapped around and text on sides, this cover design takes advantage of the negative space uniquely on each side. The text on the spine and back cover sit comfortably so it does not feel busy or overwhelming. The thickness of this book allows for stacked text on the spine, similar to the front cover.

A note about image and artwork wrapping. Be sure the artwork does not become stretched or distorted as you wrap it around. Use only photographs or artwork that has the available size to be wrapped without disrupting the front cover design.

A more minimal cover design or one that features artwork and photography that will not wrap around your spine should feature some information there instead. Keeping consistent with your front cover design here is important as to not distract or seem irrelevant.

Typography and color palette for any spine designs should remain in the same styles as your cover. As you add information around the additional cover faces, limit the number of fonts you use and be consistent with which typefaces and colors are used for headers and body text.

Maintaining the consistency with this minimal, typography based design creates a clean and professional aesthetic. The title displayed prominently on the spine will stand out on any shelf. An accent color for the spine will help this design pop without disrupting the overall style. The back cover features an airy layout with an outstanding call to the reader utilizing the title font with an easy to read summary.

Similar to the guidelines for the spine, you'll want to plan your back cover design based on if you'd like to wrap the image or artwork completely. Consistency again here is key to giving your book a professionally designed feel. Including text on your back cover is important but do not over-include. A short summary, a review, and a short blurb about the author. Maybe a photo if you're feeling particularly photogenic, or if the other top sellers in your genre are including it. Follow their lead, but there's not need to include anything beyond the minimum. A design can easily be crowded an overwhelming and cause people to shy away from your book.

A cover design that features photography or artwork on the front but does not wrap around must be supported by a clean and consistent spine and back cover. Maintaining the tone and color of your image throughout your design is important to create a uniform and clean look. An author photo and bio on the back cover is widely popular in the self-help and non-fiction genres. If you are including a photo, take the time to make sure it is a good one that will represent you professionally.

A wrapped artwork design featuring a text box on the back cover. The background artwork would make placing legible text on top incredibly challenging. The text box allows you to separate your description, reviews, bio, or anything else that would get lost in the background.

Incorporating your color and typography on the back cover can be a little trickier but there are a few general guidelines that you can follow to get a cleaner and more professional design.

• Use your header typeface and color no more than twice. This will be the first thing peoples eyes will jump to and using it everywhere is only distracting. The standard places are top of your back cover summary and a review.

• Increase line spacing for your summary, author bio, and reviews. Legibility on the back is key and you'll only have a few seconds of their attention so make it as easy as possible for your audience to take it all in. Avoid using all capital letters in the body text.

• If you want to wrap your imagery or artwork but your text doesn't read well over it, consider creating a text box that sits above the background. This will legibly separate your text while allowing you to utilize the wrap-around design.

The final pieces you'll have to include on your back cover are the usual: barcode, ISBN, ASIN, and publishing information. This typically nestles neatly at the bottom of the cover but it never hurts to give it some space.

Oh my! Was that the sixth step? Yes it was! That can only mean one thing: just one more little chapter to send you on your way with your new, fancy book cover.

DONE AND DONE-R

Almost done, I promise. Just a few finishing details and you will be good to go! It is important to give credit where credit is due so be sure that any artwork, imagery, and typefaces that you choose. Even if you found it for free online doesn't mean that you're free to use it commercially. These designers, developers, and artists spent a lot of time and energy creating these resources, just as you did planning, writing, and editing you book. In many cases, the artists that you collaborate with will be more than willing to negotiate their rates and share your book featuring their art or type once you've released. This can open up a massive, new market to increase your reach and sell more copies. But the whole marketing aspect we'll have to save for another book.

Ahh… let it breathe. Make sure all your text has enough space around the outside edge of the cover. Many printers ask for design files that are slightly larger than the actual cover. This excess area is called the bleed and will be trimmed off after they print it. If you are including an image or artwork that you want to extend to the edges of the cover, make sure that this is to the edge of the bleed. Some of it will be trimmed but it will ensure a clean, fully printed cover. The text is what we don't want to lose. This area is referred to as the margin, and varies by printer but is usually 1/4". You need to give this some good space so it doesn't get lost in the cut.

A little visualization for your bleed, trim, and safe area. Starting with Fig. 1, bleed: this is the dark grey area surrounding your cover. Any artwork, photos, or colors that you want to extend to the edge of your cover design should go to the outer edge of your bleed.

Fig. 2, trim: the middle, lighter grey are. The outer line of the trim section is where your book cover will actually be cut. As some printers and trimmers are slightly off, they like to leave a little padding around these areas for safety.

Fig. 3, safe area or margin, the center area. All of your text, barcodes, and other important information should remain within this space.

Your printer and book dimensions will affect the measurements of each of these spaces, so be sure to research it beforehand!

A few years ago, someone told me something that I try to apply to everything I do now. *Done is better than perfect.* It seems so simple but getting caught up in chasing perfection will ruin any hopes of getting your book to market. Perfection may exist for certain things but is the time investment to find it, worth it? If you are struggling to find a design that you are happy with, you can always start again, follow a new path, make a few different decisions and you might come up with something you never even thought of. But, don't get stuck in the mud of perfection. Get it done, put it out there, and sell a million copies!

These steps are the basic rules that I follow for each one of my designs and they've been good to me so far. I wanted to share them with you because I do believe that you can visualize and create your own unique book cover that is smart and effective. Utilize the tools and resources that surround you and build on them.

Thank you for reading, I hope you have an awesome book cover from using this guide or at least learned a few things along the way! I love to see what people come up with so please don't hesitate to send me your designs, ideas, and questions. Thanks again!